The use of too many questions has been avoided, as it is more important to encourage comment and discussion than to expect particular answers.

Care has been taken to retain sufficient realism in the illustrations and subject matter to enable a young child to have fun identifying objects, creatures and situations.

It is wise to remember that patience and understanding are very important, and that children do not all develop evenly or at the same rate. Parents should not be anxious if children do not give correct answers to those questions that are asked. With help, they will do so in their own time.

The brief notes at the back of this book will enable interested parents to make the fullest use of these **Ladybird talkabout** books.

Ladybird Books Loughborough

compiled by W. Murray

illustrated by Harry Wingfield

The publishers wish to acknowledge the assistance of
the nursery school advisers who helped with the
preparation of this book,
especially that of Lady Britton, Chairman,
and Miss M Puddephat, M Ed, Vice Chairman
of The British Association for Early Childhood
Education (formerly The Nursery School Association).

talkabout
animals

What noise does each one make ?

Tell the story

1

3

5

Say what the animals are, which are black and which are white

Talk about the picture and what the cat and kittens are doing

Where does each one sleep?

Tell the story

Tell the 'long dog' story!

Big and little

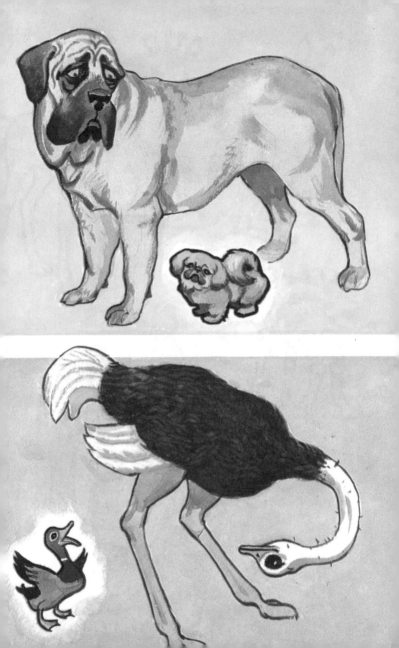

Match each
animal with
its black shape

Tell the story

Which food does each animal eat?

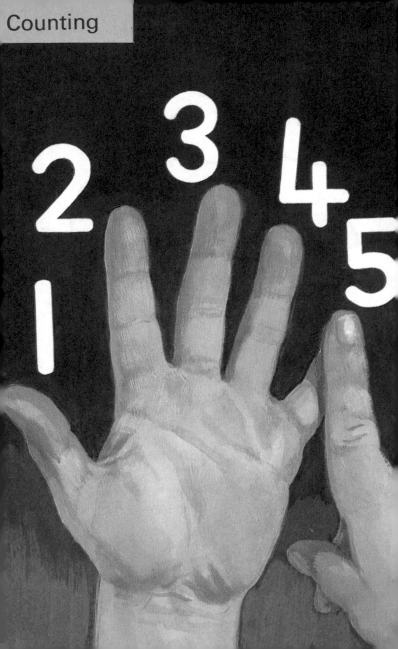

Say what the animals are, which are slow and which are fast

1

4

2

3

5

Tell the story

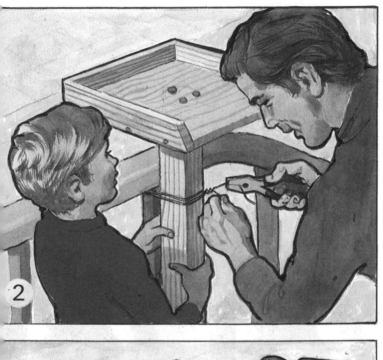

LOOK and find
another like this

and this

and this

Which
picture
matches
this one ?

and this one ?

and this one ?

Talk about sheep and wool

Their wool keeps them warm and we use it to keep **us** warm.

Feel the softness and warmth of wool in a rug, a coat or a scarf.

Suggestions for extending the use of this **talkabout** book . . .

The page headings are only brief suggestions as to how the illustrations can be used. However, these illustrations have been planned to help children understand various important concepts during their discussions with you. For example, you can talk about the **large** and **small** animals or birds in the first picture, pointing out that some are **parents** and some are their **young,** that a parent bird is perched **over** the nest, that the nest is **under** it, that the ducks are floating **on** the water, etc. All these concepts are essential to a child's increasing understanding and vocabulary.

In many of the illustrations (particularly, for example, the 'Look and find another like this' and 'Match each animal with its black shape') visual differences of shape and colour can be pointed out. The ability to